Mommy is not GOD

By: **Carra Dixon**

Copyright © 2020

All rights reserved. No portion of this book may be reproduced in any form without permission from the publisher, except as permitted by U.S. copyright law. For permissions request write to the publisher addressed "Attention Permission Coordinator"

authorcarradixon@gmail.com

ISBN: 978-0-578-76004-9

Ordering Information: *For information about special discounts available for bulk purchases, sales promotions, fund-raising and educational needs, contact the Author at the above email.*

Prologue

This book is a look into the emotional and passionate relationship between mother and daughter. Women who say that they can't get along with other women usually adopt that type of attitude from their first female encounter which is the mother-daughter relationship. As black women we are taught to be strong, and independent. We learn to do what we can for our family and we do it with little or no help. We suffer in silence but smile in public just to survive the day. The title of this book is a contradiction; but it's also a perfect description of what goes on behind the scenes of a not so good relationship. I do believe all of us women are Gods and Goddess. We have nature, a spirit, and a being that can't be explained and that is God-like at times. We also have to take note and remember too that we make mistakes and are all still human. Some of these mistakes can be fixed, changed and improved overtime. But some of these mistakes have lasting effects that may not be as easily resolved.

I have had a difficult relationship with my mother and that is the basis for this book. I know that I'm not alone with the relationship dynamics shared between me and my mother. I also want to talk about the relationships that contribute to our relationship such as the one between her and her mother. The generational curse of a difficult mother-daughter relationship affects a lot of us but we often get shamed for talking about it. We get ridiculed for feeling negative thoughts about our mother. We are told too many cliche phrases about how to treat and respect our mother. My relationship with my mother is not the worst of the worst but it definitely could be so much better. I have seen and heard of worse. I know that this is something that needs to be discussed openly without shame or guilt. I too am a mother so I know both sides to the story. As a daughter there is no way I should be made to feel bad simply for the way I feel. I shouldn't be ashamed of how I have been treated by anyone, especially my mother. These thoughts and feelings do not take away the love or appreciation of anything she has done for me; nor how much she means to me.

Mommy is not God is an eye-opener into something that has been kept silent. Hopefully, it will create a forum for those who have something to express without being shamed for it.

"If you didn't come from a healthy family, make sure a healthy family comes from you_ Unknown"

Dedication

This book is dedicated to that woman who sits alone and cries about a relationship that is out of your control. She tries to balance everything in her life but knows that in the back of her mind something is not right. She feels like no one understands what she is going through. She loves another woman (her mother) but also hates her. She is bothered by her, she is made to feel guilty about the way she feels and she's unsure how to handle her emotions. This is for those who are told " you only get one mother". This is for the woman who gets looked at as the bad child knowing they did nothing wrong or that a relationship is a two-way street.

This book is dedicated to all the sub mothers out there. My aunts, my mother in law, my mother's friends, my friends mothers, and my neighbors who played the role of a mother when I needed it most. These women really don't know how much of an impact they made in my life on a day to day basis.

When they say that it takes a village to raise a child that is a fact but the village is not often recognized or acknowledged for the job that they are doing. So I want to send appreciation and recognize all the women who are making a difference in young women's lives. Continue to be that role model, hero, or savior. Be that listening ear, that shoulder to cry on, or that guidance when asked.

My book is of course dedicated to my mother. Without her, I wouldn't have a book. We don't have the best relationship and that is ok. Everything I talk about in this book is my opinion, my feelings and my point of view. That does not mean that it is written in stone, that does not mean my feelings and opinions can not be changed. It is simply what I am going through, how I feel and what I have learned. My mother and I can get better or can stay the same and fester. Like with every relationship I hope it will grow. Writing this book has been a big part of my growth and has been a great experience. I hope that everyone who reads it takes something from it and grows. We are all entitled to our feelings and opinions so let no one tell you otherwise or make you feel bad for it. A relationship with your mother can be a very complex relationship. Don't let the toxicity take over your life. Your mental health and happiness come first. Love you, Mommy.

> *"Motherhood: all love begins and ends there_Robert Browning"*

Mommy Is Not God **poem by Ayanna Dixon**

There was a time in my life,

Where I thought my mom was God

I thought she could do anything

Be here, Be there, even climb mount everest

There was a time when I thought,

"My mom is invincible"

I thought she was a superhero

And could always save the day.

But as I started to grow I realized that

Mommy is not God!

I started to realize that mommy had flaws,

And that she made mistakes

I realized that sometimes she cries

And sometimes she's not having a good day

But in the end I will always have something to say

About my mother always being there for me.

Chapter 1

When I was young I used to think that my mother was the best person in the world. As many of us do we believe that Mommy is God. I was dependent on her every move and her every breath. I loved being around her all the time. I loved being with her no matter what she was doing or where she was. I could only imagine that this is how most if not all children are at the beginning of life. My mommy was the light of my life as a baby. My mommy was my everything. I couldn't eat without Mommy. Couldn't sleep without Mommy. We come to depend on our mommy to make the right decisions in our life. Of course, I can't really remember being a baby but we all know how mommy and baby relationships should go. We know when you have a baby that you are solely responsible for your babies every want and need. We do have secondary and other guardians that are in the picture but no one role is as important as mommy.

When I got a little older I would sit in the bar with my mom and I would eat crabs with her and all of her friends. They all adored me. Back then it was ok to take a child into a bar, especially the neighborhood bar where everyone knows everyone. Being the only child I would definitely receive special treatment from everyone who knew her. I would miss her when she was gone. I would light up with joy when she returned from wherever she went. I remember throughout my years of being with my mom I was able to get all the things that I wanted. I wasn't a very demanding child. I didn't really want or need much but I was very spoiled.

Being a child and not knowing what Mommy was really into or what she was doing I thought she could do no wrong. Even when I ended up in foster care and eventually the custody of my paternal grandmother I still thought Mommy was perfect. When my mom would visit I still got excited and didn't want her to leave. She would bring me toys and clothes and I just loved it. At the time I didn't think much about how and why I was living with my grandma and not my mommy. But I stayed there until I was about 10 or 11 years old. When I moved back in with my mommy I was a little older but still naive to what she did and who she really was. I still had that Godly image of my mommy. I would believe everything she said. I would cook for her not really knowing what I was doing but when I went knocking on her door she wouldn't be there. I would "lend" her money and never get it back. I know you are probably thinking that is my mother and if she needed the money just give it to her. Like I said I was young so when she said she would give it back I believed her. The little birthday money that I would save quickly gone. My expensive toys or gifts would end up missing and I didn't understand at the time why. She was no longer the fun energetic happy Mother that I thought I knew. She was more distant, quiet and seemed mean to me. She seemed to care more about her partners and friends than me. I would do little things that were out of my character and barely get in trouble for them.

Being raised by my grandmama gave me more sense than most of the children growing up around me. She exposed me to a lot and kept me grounded and educated. So if it wasn't for her I would have been way worse due to what I experienced when living with Mommy. I started to not care about things because it didn't seem like my mom cared about them. So in school I never did my homework or just did the bare minimum. I ended up failing the 6th grade and having to repeat it with younger kids. The one good thing that came out of that is I met the love of my life and we eventually married and had 3 kids. I would do little things in school and when I got in trouble I would only be on punishment for about a day or two. My punishment consisted of no phone or outside play or television. This really didn't bother me because I was pretty much a loner that preferred to read books, listen to music or write. The punishments didn't affect me at all. Like I said if it wasn't for my grandma and already having standards about life I would have done way worse. It was all to get attention from my mom but it didn't really work. Failing the 6th grade I realized I was only hurting myself. You can't expect anyone to care more about you than yourself if that makes sense.

When I finally became old enough to understand why my mother was the way she was I guess it was a bit of a shock. She was a drug addict and alcoholic. She started coming home high and actually talking to me about it. That scared the shit out of me and kinda left a scar.

What do you do with that type of information as a child? She really told me that her heart could explode any minute because she just did what was called an 8ball. I realized my borrowed money was buying the things she needed to stay high. My keyboard that she bought for me was in a pawn shop somewhere. The days she was not around when I cooked for her she was elsewhere getting high. Realizing that my mommy was not this perfect woman hurt me to the core. Feeling like I was her last priority because that street life meant so much to her killed me. Her first tattoo she got was the name of her partner. Not her one and only child but someone she didn't know if she was going to be with today or tomorrow. It was the little things like this that took a big toll on my mental and emotional state.

I was left in the house to take care of myself on a regular basis. Her friends that I would call aunt and uncle took care of me more than she did. We moved from house to house apartment to apartment and it was no fun. Mostly in the same neighborhood so I didn't have to change schools, which was a good thing.

As an adult now and a mother who's a recovering alcoholic I guess I kinda understand more about what life put you through and how some people handle it. I was neglected and ignored and forced to grow up fast and make mature decisions. I think the biggest hurt is my mother never admitting how our life really was. She's the type that doesn't like to confront things that will cause hurt. She likes to pretend that everything is ok. When I hear stories from the past from my childhood I get different versions from different people. Now my mom says she didn't start using drugs until I was taken away from her as if that was the trigger. That may be true but my Godmom told me that when I was a baby she took care of me because Mommy was always out and about. She may not have been doing drugs but she was in the bars and didn't care too much for me. After all, I did end up in DHS custody and foster care. I still don't know the facts surrounding why I was taken away and how I ended up living with my Grandmother.

My mother and her Mother also have and always had a difficult relationship. But they put a band-aid over it and pretend nothing ever happened. This is the dysfunction cycle that I can't or won't do. Not just because I don't drink anymore but because I feel like that is so fake and doesn't solve anything. The version of the DHS story was told to me by my Mom-Mom and that is the only version I know. Apparently my Mom-Mom was fed up with keeping me one day and just decided to take me into the bar that my mom worked at and told her that she wasn't keeping me anymore. How that transpired to DHS involvement I am not sure. I do want more answers to my questions but bringing up the past and emotional situations with those two is like pulling teeth. They will dance all around the questions and may not answer with the truth. Then it will turn into a big argument about who is telling the truth or why do I want to know. I just feel like it's pointless to talk to them most of the time, especially on topics that are real.

I am now 33 years old and finally getting my voice back when it comes to standing up to my mom and Mom-Mom. Mom-Mom has a habit of talking to everyone as if they are children. My mom gets upset and emotional whenever someone is saying something she doesn't like. This makes it very hard to have conversations or disagreements with either of them. I had to be the parent a lot of the time when it comes to the relationship with my mom and her behaviors. My mom has temper tantrums and I'm forced to calm her down or talk her out of a suicide attempt. Looking back I know she wouldn't have killed herself, it's just her way of getting attention and the drugs and alcohol makes it even worse. The last time she had a tantrum I refused to tolerate it. I had to literally treat her like a child and cuss her out. After that she stopped. What child should have to go through that adult or not? Don't get me wrong I don't sit around and feel sorry for myself about what I have been through. I actually appreciate it for the most part. I truly believe everything happens for a reason. If Mommy wasn't the way she was I would have never ended up with my Grandmother. I am proud to say I passed on the values and beliefs to my children and others that my Grandmother instilled in me. My mommy is of a different breed in connection to being raised by an older woman. Her Mother is more toxic than she is and makes me believe this is the reason she still acts like a child, she still is an alcoholic and she still stray away from reality. She is not an honest person there has been so many times when I have caught her in a lie and she would laugh it off as if it was a joke. She is manipulative. I have seen her treat people in such a loving manner until she gets what she wants and afterwards they are not useful to her and she shows it. She is mean to my children but only behind the scenes then denies it when it is brought to light. My mother and I have a lot of things to talk about and issues to mend in order to have a functional relationship. I guess it is my job to bring this to her attention if I want this relationship to go anywhere or grow. My only question is with a Mother like mine is it worth the time and effort or do I just move on?

> *"You can give them another chance, or you can forgive let go, and give yourself a better chance_Unknown"*

Chapter 2

I think it is easy for me to empathize with a lot of people and what they have been through in life that made them how they are. I feel like that is what makes me a people person. It makes me non judgemental. It contributes to the diverse group of friends that I have had in school and have now. I know that no one is like the next person in every way. I can say that I am good at forgiving and forgetting when I have been hurt. I have done it time and time again. But for some strange reason these same understandings and values that I have don't apply to my relationship with my mother. The Mother and Daughter dynamics for me has more emotion behind it and not much logic. What I mean is I feel a way when it comes to my mother. Since she was put on this pedestal by me she should fulfill it with no questions asked. It's not logical to think that way. My heart is telling me that this is true but my mind knows damn well this is not reality. I get my feelings hurt and my mental state is so affected because I can't put my feelings aside long enough to analyze our relationship to make sense to me.

As I sit here and write this book she is demanding my attention and I feel like I just wasted 20 minutes of work. Of course she doesn't know what I am doing, she just believes that what she needs is important and I should be ready and willing to help her when it's needed. My mom seems to have the perception of a best friend relationship between me and her but I don't see it that way. I do admit it's not often I confront her to show her otherwise. I couldn't be friends with someone who acts one way in my face and another way when I am not around. My mother will look me right in the face and lie for her own selfish gain or to prevent being called out. I used to do the same things when I was younger. When I matured I realized that lying is a waste of energy and time.

My mother has never matured and I can partially see why. Her mother who I call *"Mom-Mom"* treats everyone as if they are a child. She treats everyone as if they are less than. I believe she thinks they know nothing and she knows everything. I can kind of understand why my mom turned out the way that she did. It is a lot of pressure to put on a person to be this perfect being at all times. And Mom-Mom expects perfection.

In relation to the fact that us women are very emotional creatures and love hard and fight harder I believe this causes the mother daughter relationship to be ten times as hard. We love so hard that when we get hurt an automatic wall goes up and we are taught to hate just as hard. Not on purpose but once we are hurt we no longer want that feeling so we do what we know to prevent it from happening again, that usually takes on the form of anger. We have been shown to take on a bad attitude and not trust anymore. We as women and especially black women have not been taught to deal with our emotions in an unhealthy way. When we are hurt we shut down or even retaliate. We know longer have a positive thought about those who have hurt us. It's like the saying goes, *"Hurt people Hurt people"* I feel like a lot of this goes into play when it comes to our mental health.

"Hurt people! Hurt people!"

Chapter 3

Let's talk about mental health and the connection with relationships for a minute. Lately I have been seeing a therapist. I have been suffering from depression, anxiety, ptsd, and having panic attacks. Yeah that's a lot I know. Of course one of the topics we tend to touch on is my mother. Now my therapist tells me that I am justified for feeling the way I feel towards my mother. I have also gotten confirmation from another doctor who's podcast I listen to. I guess my issue is that I don't like having ill feelings about anyone. Of course my mother is the last person I would want to feel like I just don't want around me. I mean when she calls my name my face automatically frowns up. I am a happy person who loves to love. I have been through a lot and have been hurt again and again. For some reason I always let her get to me emotionally.

Since I started going to therapy I have improved with managing my emotions. So I've been speaking my peace with her lately instead of just letting things go. Of course when I do confront her she is full of lies and pleas. That doesn't stop me because I am now at the point where I am just fed up with the child-like attitude. I am mentally exhausted from her acting like a baby some days, being mean and nasty to my children when I am not around, yet all smiles and butterflies when she's in my face. She claims she suffers from bipolar depression and some other mental issues. I can believe that but not too extreme that she claims. In my therapy session I have learned that I have to care about myself first. I have to speak up when it is necessary. I still have a hard time determining when that is. If it is not life or death I'm usually like "oh well". What I do know is that

I can no longer let my mom get away with acting as a child.

A lot of what I have been through is now finally taking a toll on my mental health for various reasons. I am quick to ignore people's flaws and make excuses for the way they treat me. I turn their negativity into my problem that I need to fix within myself and most likely by myself. I carry other people's baggage around in my heart. I feel bad for hurting feelings even if I don't intend to. My mother has a lot of issues dealing with mental health that also stems from growing up with her Mother's hurt. This does not justify the way she treats others or her behaviour. Causing emotional damage to your child is something you don't want to do but once it is brought to your attention and you chose to do nothing to change it is when the relationship usually turns sour. Carrying this heavy weight and blaming myself while holding it all in could have literally driven me crazy. It has damaged me emotionally but also made me resilient. I put these feelings aside and now being self aware as an adult realize the damage it has caused.

My mom's negativity was something that she didn't hide or try to explain. So when she was upset about anything it showed. As a child I would take it personal because I felt like she was mad at me. I couldn't comprehend at that time that my mom had a life outside of being a Mother so her emotional state did not always have anything to do with me. I took everything my mom did personal because I didn't know any better. I didn't know that the world didn't revolve around me. This now plays a huge role in how I respond to people when they are upset. My insecurities always make me feel like the cause of others disappointment is because of me. I now have to remind myself as an adult that other people have feelings and experiences tribulations that are not necessarily influenced by my presence.

As a mother I try to communicate with my children at age appropriate level what it is that I'm going through and why. I have explained to my oldest daughter all about my mental health and the challenges with my depression so she understands it's not related to her doing or lack thereof. My daughter loves to be around me and when I am feeling the symptoms of my depression I like to keep away from my children so that I don't let my negative attitude affect them. I would never want them to think they are the cause of my anger or sadness. I can't always remove myself or catch my mental changes around them but I try. The emotions displayed while in the home will set the tone for the whole family. So when I am upset for whatever reason it makes for a miserable family and bad experiences.

It was only me and my mother for the most part so all of her negative vibes affected me. This was not fun. Being the only child and not having someone to talk to and share my problems with or someone who could relate and help me deal with all of what was going on was very difficult. I didn't have anyone who could comfort which formed guilt. The guilt set in because I knew I was the cause of someone else's misery and despair. I felt guilty for a lot of what my mother went through with her being sad and or angry all the time behind closed doors. This guilt that I felt for ruining my mother's mood would cause me to overcompensate for things I didn't do. Due to this I turned into a people pleaser. When you do something wrong and want to make up for it you do what you can to make it right. The problem with that is I did nothing wrong.

Parents use guilt to control their children a lot. Some may notice it but sometimes it's subtle and passive. For instance telling a child how much pain you were in while in labor which is not the child's fault but my mother felt that it was necessary for me to know as if she was owed something. my mother still today tries to guilt me into doing things by insinuating that she's incapable due to her age or some illness. Little does she know all she has to do is ask and most likely it will get done if I'm able to do so. I am not a person that usually tells people no but when my mother acts like a bratty four year old that wants her way I most likely don't want to do anything for her. She wants me to feel bad for her and show her pity. As a mother I probably play the guilt trip card more than I would like to or more than I even notice. My behavior is sometimes done in laughter and jokes but I know that doesnt matter if the child feels like it is the truth.

"A healthy relationship doesn't drag you down. It inspires you to be better_Mandy Hale"

Chapter 4

What does it take to make a relationship work? My opinion is that to make a relationship work is that it usually takes compromise, trust, understanding, communication, sacrifice, love and respect just to name a few. I think that most people forget that what you have with your Mother is a relationship. So most of the standards and boundaries for any relationship should apply to the mother and daughter relationship also. If your relationship with your Mother is toxic and does not appear to be getting better or bettering you as a person don't apologize for that.

My relationship with my mother does weigh on me emotionally. At one point I didn't even want to fix whatever problems we had. I just wanted to be done and get away from her for my own sanity. This is a feeling that I am not ashamed of because I've learned the importance of taking care of myself first. I want happiness and whatever relationships in my life that do not provide that I have a right to eliminate. Toxic is Toxic! No matter who or where it is coming from.

There is always something that you don't want to do but do anyway and the results or response to the action can be rewarding in some form. That to me is a compromise. Making sure that the person you are in this relationship with feels valued by doing things they like or appreciate. The action of compromise isn't necessarily for you but for the other person. Now you can receive personal enjoyment out of making someone else happy. Compromising your time, energy or maybe money to see someone else happy is not always a bad thing especially if that person is appreciative and deserving. The act of compromise does not mean to bend over backwards or deplete all that you have to give.

Trusting someone who has hurt or lied to you on so many occasions is hard. Trust for my mother has been compromised and I am not sure how she would be able to gain that back from me. She has hurt me so much that I can not trust her with my heart. I know for the most part that this hurt was not purposely done. I know that if she actually knew she has hurt me or how she has hurt me she would feel remorseful. I also know everyone gets hurt because it's a part of life. The trust really goes away once the hurt happens over and over again. Trust is also diminished when someone's actions do not match their words. This is a big part of my mother's personality and the main reason I don't trust her. She is what most would say is fake towards me and others. She will express an overwhelming loving and caring emotion towards me at times and in the same breath express anger or disapproval towards me when I am not around. So I don't trust her to be truthful all the time and especially about important topics. Trust is big to me, trust is important for a healthy relationship, and trust is what makes us grow.

My mother wants everyone to do for her when she feels it is needed and if the word NO comes out of your mouth it is a big problem for her. In return she will do whatever it is she needs to that will persuade you to comply with her only to then talk bad of you to other people. Whenever I find myself in this space I know that it's only a matter of time before my mother will remind me of why I owe her. This is not what you call a genuine act of kindness or compromise. It is a selfish way of thinking and makes me not want to ask her for anything even when she offers. .

Understanding is knowing that we are all human. We all hurt, love, bleed, cry, shit and sweat. To understand that everyone goes through things either out loud or in silence is the key to understand why a person acts and reacts the way they do. In our community and culture we are not really shown or taught the proper healthy ways to deal with hurt. The cycle just continues and no one really wins in the end. That is where communication is key. Our mental health is something we should be catering to on a daily basis. One thing that is important in relationships and helps with our mental health is communication. Now I am just starting to get back into properly communicating so I know this is a hard pill to swallow. But that relationship that is important to you needs to be an open book of dialogue. Tell them how you feel. Those who matter don't mind and those who mind don't matter. So this is truly a way of determining if the relationship is even worth being in or working on.

Now Sacrifice is give and take. I say always give 100% and expect nothing back. Let me explain. If your heart is really 100% If you always expect something in return are you really doing it from the heart or to get some type of reward. Now when I talk about relationships I am talking about any and all of them. Your mom, your child, your bestie, and your significant other. Whoever is in your life that you want or need to be there. So when you have a child you don't expect that child to respond when you say I love you or when you feed the baby to say thank you. You give all you can because you want the best for your child and you are choosing this relationship and want it to grow strong. Think of all the relationships you have this way and you will see the difference. Know you have to be willing to fight for the relationship if you see necessary. Don't get me wrong, some relationships are toxic and signs will go up to recognize this. I am speaking on the relationships you know have a meaning and a future. Don't be so quick to give up on a person. Change does take time. Also don't be afraid to change yourself.

How do you recognize a toxic relationship? I think you should follow your instincts. Not your heart because that is emotionally charged and will ignore the logic in a situation simply because of a feeling. Not your brain because that can tell you that something makes sense but it is not necessarily healthy. So that feeling in the pit of your stomach that is telling you something is not right. It tells you no matter how hard you try it won't get right. When a person makes you feel less than no matter what you do. If this relationship is shrinking instead of helping with growth. When a person is stuck in their position and is not receiving your push, motivation or encouragement as inspiration but instead see it as a negative. When that person constantly thinks you are judging them simply for stating your opinion on what is happening. That person needs to be left where they are until they are ready to grow. That relationship needs to be discontinued. It is toxic to put all your energy into something for it to go nowhere. For a relationship to succeed the energy of each person needs to somehow connect. If there is no possible match it is a toxic relationship let go. It doesn't matter who the relationship is with. It is ok to distance yourself from family. Mother will always be but you can also love your mother from a distance. As an adult you have that right.

Not every mother daughter relationship is the same. As you grow your understanding and dynamic of the relationship changes either for better or worse. Usually as a child everything is peaches and cream. As a teen you may hate your mother or be the best of friends. As an adult you try to satisfy your mother anyway possible to make her comfortable or to repay her for giving you life.

But the toxic mother daughter relationship is not talked about. It is not brought to light how damaging this very first relationship experience can be to our lives growing up. The attachment issues. The trauma. The misconception of love. The abuse mentally and sometimes physically. All of these things are learned behaviors that follow us. All of these things start when you are young. Not with the first boyfriend or first love of your life. But with your first relationship and that is Mommy and me. Usually people look at the father who is absent or the boyfriends who are not treating women like a princess. But the Mother is most responsible for the initial encounter of love and relationship. She teaches you affection. She teaches attachment, how to forgive. She teaches what is right and wrong when in a relationship.

I never got a healthy example of what a relationship should be from my mother. She went from one person to the next and never showed me stability. She would get into a lot of domestic disputes in her relationships. She was easily influenced by some or the total opposite and very controlling with others. It never seemed like pure love and affection for the most part. It was more like she just always wanted someone around for company. From this example it is hard for me to show affection and be touchy feely with my significant other. It just seems weird to me because I haven't been shown that that is normal.

She has shown me to always have someone around just in case you need them but dont keep them close they might think you want them. In a way she keeps people just close enough to use them when needed but at a distance so when she is tired of them they will not notice her distance. I tend to be somewhat needy when it comes to my husband and sometimes friends. In the same breath I don't like people around. My attachment issues cause a lot of confusion within my relationship with my husband because of this. It's like I want him to want to be around me all the time but I don't want him around all the time. Learning to love this way can really mess you up and it's hard to recognize it in yourself. That's why I am grateful my husband will bring it to my attention and I also seek therapy for these types of issues.

I lived in a small two bedroom apartment in the Logan section in Philadelphia. It was just me and Mommy. Just me and my mommy. Mommy had regained custody of me and at the time she was a little distant. I was used to being by myself due to me being an only child so it was a part of my personality. I was maybe 11 or 12 years old still in elementary school. My hobbies consist of music, writing mainly poetry, journaling and playing with my baby dolls. Living with my grandma taught me to be more efficient and independent so I did some things in the kitchen. I could of course make hot dogs and noodles. I also would cook breakfast foods a lot or just made up meals creations depending on what we had in the house. My mom was either in her room or in the streets or at work. I had everything I needed and some of what I wanted at that age. I wasn't a needy kid when it came to toys or the latest of whatever the kids had so I didn't really ask for much. I was never disappointed during Christmas or birthdays. Especially because my grandma still provided for me even though I no longer lived with her. One year I got a big keyboard in order to learn how to play the piano. I loved the keyboard even though I only knew how to play one song on it. I would make up little melodies and sing to them or add tunes to the pre recorded beats that came with the piano. I had the keyboard for a while until one day it was no longer there. Never once was I asked for the keyboard or told that it would be taken away. It just up and disappeared.

My mother sold it in order to get drugs and that was just the end of my keyboard. As a child I couldn't complain or demand another one. I just had to shut my mouth and go with it. This was a common occurrence in my house. Anything worth anything could be gone in a day and exchange for money to buy drugs.

My mother exposed me to a lot of trauma and at a young age. At the time I didn't fully understand but today as an adult I know a child should not experience seeing or hearing certain things that I did. The things that are exposed to a child should be explained on a level that they can comprehend. My mother wasn't very present due to drugs and alcohol. She was stabbed, beaten, she got into fights and we would often move from place to place. She was not very good at discipline because I got away with a lot. When I was old enough to go places on my own I was gone. She attempted suicide several times. She would throw childlike temper tantrums breaking things and crying. All of these activities put certain thoughts and feelings in me towards my mother and also took a toll on my mental state. She was no longer that sweet nurturer who gave birth to me but more like a terror.

Imagine being woken up in the middle of the night by your grandma and rushed out of the house at maybe 11 years old. I was told that my mother had been stabbed. It wasn't much details or even if she was dead or alive. I remember traces of blood on the porch as I was rushed out of the house. It was not fun. Nor being awoken to my mother crying because she was in pain from being beat in the leg with something. I couldn't help her; I did not know how so I was told to just go back to sleep. These are just some of the traumatizing experiences I had to endure before I turned 18.

Abuse is very often overlooked. Mental abuse is something that occurs very often and not even realized. My mother endured abuse mentally by her mother and physical abuse by others. She has been the abuser in some relationships both mentally and physically. I'm still not sure if what I experienced as a child would be considered mental abuse. What I do know is that I was neglected, ignored, and exposed to alot of nonsense. I can only assume that my mother had my best interest at heart but she could not control her demons to show me. I don't believe my mother truly understands the mental toll my upbringing has had on me.

"The scars you can't see are the hardest to heal_Astrid Alauda"

Chapter 5

My admiration for my mom was high when I was younger. We went through a lot but I continued adoring her. As long as I had my mom as a child all my wounds were healed temporarily. The good memories of her are her bright larger than life personality; she could be loving and fun. She knew everyone. I always had a host of Aunts and cousins who shared no blood relation and some I still have relationships with till today. Some of the relationships and bonds I formed can't be broken. My mom showed me loyalty to friends but not so much with family. My mom would call everyone baby, honey, or sweety. She knew how to sweet talk everyone in and out of any situation.

My strength is from my mother. She has dealt with a lot in her lifetime and is still here. She was raised by a mother whom she has a difficult relationship with and the toxicity problem started there.

In life many of us are not taught how to deal with things in a positive way so we use drugs and alcohol to mask the pain. Many of us don't know how to effectively communicate to actually solve issues because we are taught to just shut up and move on. Don't cry over spilled milk. So many times I hear a young black girl getting shut down or pushed away when they have a problem. Young black girl problems don't matter to many. If we actually take the time to listen and talk to one another our community would have fewer fights, crime and hate.

In my eyes, my mom was my best friend. It was mostly the two of us because my dad was locked away when I was a child. My mom always has a lady friend we would live with for a while then it would be another one. I was too young to mind or care because they all were nice and spoiled me as much if not more than my mom. Now that I look back on things I realize this is not a situation you should put a child in. There was no real stability or consistency with these relationships or our living situations.

A mother's love is usually one that can't be broken. Mother goes through so much to bear a child, to protect a child and to care for a child. From the time of pregnancy up until the child is at least 18 a mother job is never done even after the legal age of the child. A mother deals with a lot of pain and joy. Motherhood is a rollercoaster that you can never imagine if you don't experience it. Not all mothers do a supreme job but I believe if you are trying your best that's a start. Once this child is grown and gets a better understanding of life then it will become clear that we are all human. Once we become older we realize that our Mothers are human and make mistakes also. The God-like image fades with maturity and an understanding of life. Though there is no handbook on raising children; at what point does a Mother become aware of the damage she caused and corrects it? If you have experienced similar things like I have it's important to know that YOU can break a generational curse.

As a mother I want to protect, love and raise my children to be the best version of themselves. I want them to be better than me. I want them to know I will always be there but they also have to know how to survive without me. I want so much for my children and a lot of the time it is hard to actually see these things through while dealing with my own demons. One thing that I do pride myself on is that I try to explain these things to my children. I try to get them to understand as much of life as they can at an early age.

Being raised by my grandma taught me to be kind to all. She taught me forgiveness and understanding. My grandma was old school, pro black, empowering and respected. Education was everything and not just school; self education and world education was important also. So this actually is a big part of my parenting now. I teach my children to be self sufficient. I teach them the things that they will actually need in life to survive. I teach them if you don't know, look it up. My children are still young; 8, 11, and 13. My 13 yr old has a job that helps with career choices. All my children cook, clean and wash clothes. Not like little slaves or anything but they know how and why these things are important to life. They see that I just don't tell them to do things for the sake of doing them. I also partake in these house chores so that I'm not only telling but showing them some tools needed for self sufficiency. I make sure to provide structure and consistency because it was lacking for me in my childhood. show and tell them what is important and how to survive on their own. My mother was more laid back and carefree. She tried to be more of a friend than a mother even though that's not what I needed. Friendship with a child should come more towards grown up years after you finish raising them if that is what you really want. I believe that children need boundaries and limits to understand that it's a time and place for everything.

A part of my mother's discipline when I would show out or act up would be to punish me but it never stuck. The punishment would last maybe a day or two. I didn't learn any lessons. If anything I would disobey the punishment and just still do whatever I wanted. Thank God I wasn't a ruthless child. I was a bit scared and too much of a leader not a follower so my acting up wasn't too bad. I would maybe get in trouble for talking too much in school, not doing school work, or being late to school. Oh yeah and playing with fire I was a bit of a pyromaniac. My mother wasn't consistent so I did these things often not caring about her day or two of no tv, no phone and no outside. What did I care about everyone I talked to went to school with me and tv never really interested me anyway. I stopped caring because I felt like she didnt care. Boy was that a big mistake. I had to repeat the 6th grade due to my lack of care.

All I wanted is for my mother to pay me some attention like I perceived she did when I was younger. I wanted when I was younger to truly feel like the child and not the parent. I envision this pretty painted portrait of the mother daughter relationship on the outside but inside is the pain. My pain came from my relationship with her and my father. I'm not sure where my mother's pain came from. What I do know is that it pains me to know that she hurts and I can't help. I imagine that my mother must feel the same way about me as her only child.

My mom was poisoned. Poisoned by this world and by her mother. Realizing Mommy is not God was hard to admit to myself. I feel like my mother has allowed life and everything to poison her and change her from the loving woman she once was. I feel like I've been let down by her and I still take it personally. As much as I try to forget the wounds don't completely heal.

At what point in our relationship did I go from adoring her to resenting her? I was blind to all my mother's flaws for so long. What changed? I had images in my mind, head and heart that were not 100% true about her. The heart needs to hold malicious intent in order for me to turn away from a person.

My admiration for my mother turned to disappointment once her bad habits outweighed the good. She would make promises and not keep them. She would disappear for days. She would sell things out of the house. She would come home high and act crazy. She would threaten to kill herself. The consistency of being inconsistent was something that I didn't quite understand. She was supposed to make sure I didn't get hurt but I was being hurt by her. She consistently let me down. She even left me at a pizza shop one day and I had to walk to my Mom's Mom's house. I was the one who got in trouble for it because supposedly she told me to stay there and she would be back. I never heard her tell me to stay put. I just knew she left and it took her too long to get back. So I decided to walk to the nearest house I knew of but all hell broke loose. My Mom-Mom was mad at my mom and my mom was mad at me. I wasn't sure what I did wrong but I was terrified. I remember my mother yelling at me in anger when we got home. She even went so far as to smash a glass with her fist on the table and I was shaken. I knew how to hide my emotions very well back then. Plus being young

I could pretty much forget my home life when I got to school. If I was out with my friends or watching tv and even when I put my head in a book, it would take me to another place in my mind. My favorite way to escape was always writing. I would write my mother poems for mothers day and she would love them. I stayed with a journal and wrote in it regularly. Writing was always my therapy.

When children are young they find outlets to deal with their mental problems. They are not sure how to deal with certain feelings. They are not sure how to express what they really want to say or do. A child's coping mechanism can be positive, or negative. It can be internal or external. It can be delayed or an immediate reaction. For me I internalized and hid my emotions. Therefore my mental state was delayed and I have to deal with them as an adult. I wasn't a child that carried around a bad attitude. I did not act out to an extreme that would land me into real trouble. I simply kept a smile on my face. I laughed. I joked. I was always in a good spirit. But that didn't reflect what was deep inside me. This is how I learned to handle my emotions because this is what I saw. My mom was in pain and you could tell by her home life. She stayed by herself. She had meltdowns and suicide attempts. But to everyone outside she was the life of the party. She was always smiling. I admired the way my mother carried herself. You know the saying: never let them see you sweat. I saw that as a strength and subconsciously mocked it.

"Being a mother is learning about strengths you didn't know you had, and dealing with fears you didn't know existed_Linda Wooten"

Chapter 6

Learning how to love is the first lesson in life you get from your mother. Although the lessons that you get is usually blamed on your adult relationships. If you are broken and handling it wrong it gets blamed on the man or boy who hurt you. Sometimes the relationship with our mother is what causes attachment issues. We spend so much time in our mother's presence and don't want to let go. Like with our mate we may become uneasy and trust issues arise and paranoia may set in. Getting spoiled by our mothers teaches us to depend on someone else and is hard to break. I've experienced this as a mother and as a daughter. I know that not everyone has this attachment presented with their child rather because of postpartum or some type of addiction. Some of us never learned how to love and we continue to imitate what we see. Now this child may get into relationships and not know how to show affection towards their mate. These issues will continue on in every relationship especially the one with your mate; I've experienced these issues. My mother was always loving and affectionate but I was also abandoned by her. So I do have attachment issues but at the same time I put a wall up and believe that this will prevent me from getting hurt from someone. I can now see how my defense mechanism I have developed to cope has made it difficult for some to get close to me. There are so many events that I can contribute to why I am the way I am in regards to loving someone else but I'm now more focused on recognizing and correcting these issues to maintain healthy relationships. Now married I have learned how to be vulnerable, trusting, and dependent on someone else. This is still not an easy task for me but I'm learning.

Due to my abandonment it has developed in me a lack of trust of others. I can recall being in foster care and having a family that could take care of me but they made the decision to get rid of me. This and other instances made me believe I was not worth keeping or fighting for. Being taken away from my mother made me wonder constantly; if my mother doesn't fight for me who will? Today I don't make a big fuss over any aspect of my life due to my lack of trust in people. I did not want to have a traditional wedding. I did not understand nor was I excited to be the center of attention. Being someone focus is still unusual to me and does not make me feel good. I did not feel like people were there to celebrate such a joyous moment that was important to me I felt like they just wanted to party. Though I know this thinking is not correct and I'm so appreciative of everyone that was in attendance my paranoia was high during this time.

The feeling of me wanting to be around someone at all times is also a problem. I believe those around me should know what I want at all times because all my good memories my mom knew what I wanted. This is such a far fetched concept that I've created in my mind and I know it. Logically it does not make sense. Emotionally, it makes perfect sense to me. So can you see the dilemma here?

"We accept the love we think we deserve_Stephen Chbosky"

Chapter 7

A mother raises a child the best that she can with or without input and knowledge from others. Some mothers make mistakes and believe that they do not have to correct any of their wrongdoings. More mothers should be open to listen more and receive the help and feedback that's needed. As an adult who is now aware of my shortcomings as a person and as a mother I try to correct in me what was broken by others.

After listening to a quote by *Will Smith* I realized that it's not my fault that I was broken or hurt but it's now my responsibility to fix it to make it better. I have learned to give all of the weight from my past to whom it belongs too. If I continue to hold my pain and hurt in how will my mother know that she has hurt me. As far as she knows she did her best and she convinced herself that I'm ok. Our relationship is good in her eyes and she doesn't see the many nights I cry in my room alone. She doesn't see me get upset and frowns my face when something happens between us. All she knows is what she sees. It is my responsibility to give her the baggage of my childhood due to her parenting. People only know what you show them or tell them. Being as though I am good at hiding my true feelings most people believe I am mentally stable most of the time. Just recently I have been vulnerable but not with the most important people that need to know the pain they caused. It is hard to do so because I don't trust them to react in a way that would actually make the situation better.

    Abuse and neglect is a big problem when dealing with parenting. It is often ignored or misunderstood. I wouldn't think or say that I was abused at all but neglected was a feeling I got a lot. It is hard for me to understand as a mother and a child the decision to have someone else raise your child. Now from what I know it was my mom Mom who started the process by saying she was unfit to raise me. If this was not true I don't see why I wasn't returned to my mother. Now the fact that I was with my grandmother for about 8 to 10 years tells me that my mother's number one priority was not to get her life together in order to regain custody of me. I was taken away from her and she was accused of wrongdoing but she did not defend herself or protect me. Thank God for my Grandma who stepped in and took responsibility for a child that was not her own. The feeling of not being wanted or not loved as I should have been is something that has been at the back of my mind my entire life. I'm pretty sure you can understand why. Being that young I didn't fully understand how and why a mother could let this happen. How can you let anything come between you and your child? Or why would you allow your personal activities to become more important than raising your own child.

Being given up on at a young age had me to believe that no one wanted me. If they did want me then they would eventually leave or hurt me. I took everything personal as if the world revolved around me and I was the reason or cause for human actions towards me. My significant other who is now my husband along with some therapy helped me to realize that this isn't true. I am not a victim of other people's thoughts, feelings, or problems. When someone is upset around me I automatically assume it is my fault. Well now I know these things are not true but it took me a while to admit it and realize everyone has their own misfortunes. I have been paranoid about whether or not someone liked me as long as I can remember. I didn't consider the fact of people not knowing how to deal with feelings, thoughts, and bad times and that it often gets mistaken for just having a bad attitude or being hateful.

Hate! I have always said hate was a strong word. I try my best to keep it out of my vocabulary. I very seldom use it when speaking about a person and it would be contradictory to say it about a person you love. So to actually hear someone speak that way about a mother or a daughter it hurts my heart. I have prayed or wished death on people plenty of times. Unfortunately one of these people is my mother. At that point in my life I was very heart broken and in a deep depression. Suffering from PTSD, anxiety and panic attacks. I had just recently lost another mother who happens to be my mother in law while mourning the death of my grandmother years later. These women hurt me in a way I didnt know was possible. They left me. I remember wishing it was my own birth mother at the time. It scared me that something like that would pop in my head. With a few sessions with my therapist I realized that it was pretty normal and ok to think that way. It was frightening to admit those thoughts. I know it is selfish to think this way and impossible for some to believe because my mother is not the devil but she is the cause of my hurt. I often wonder why couldn't she be different or better for me. I've come to the conclusion that we all have flaws. So the real problem is not what she did or didn't do; the problem is how I learn to accept it and move on. I'm learning to deal with the hurt so that I am not bitter or resentful. I don't hate anyone! I selfishly believed that by wishing death it would erase the pain for me. So my thoughts and feelings were based off of my bitterness and anger that I am learning to deal with.

"Darkness cannot drive out darkness: only light can do that. Hate cannot drive out hate: only love can do that_Martin Luther King Jr."

Chapter 8

I have witnessed worse relationships than the one my mother and I have. I have seen mothers treat their daughters like pure crap. So I learned to be grateful our encounter was not as bad as it could be. Our relationship may not have been how I wanted it to be but it was needed to become the woman I am today. It was needed to help others. It was needed to make me stronger for the next generation of girls and women who come after me. I try to take everything as a lesson to make me better and to be a better mother. I just hope that I can get past my pass to make a better future.

My Mom-Mom obviously has a lot to do with the way my mother is. She seems sweet at times. She seems to want to help people. She seems so caring. But when she doesn't get things her way or feel as if you are not doing what she says and how she wants you to do it then a monster comes out. She treats all 3 of her adult children as if they are 8 years old and only she knows what is best for them. She is money hungry and doesn't respect anyone else's opinion. She is the short little old lady who is always loud. I guess her mouth makes her feel big. We do not get along very much because she can't buy me and I can't be manipulated by her. I also refuse to sit with the two pretending everything is ok and drink until I can't remember anything. They have a fake relationship that is toxic and is very confusing. My mother seems to only discuss how much she dislikes her mother when she doesn't buy her alcohol or when money is involved. I have witnessed those two be so mean and nasty to each other verbally and the next day fake laugh with each other over some drinks and cigarettes. It is sickening to watch. My Mom-Mom is lonely. She seems to think that if she buys you things you want you will sit and talk with her. But she dont want to have real conversations about real life issues. They like to sit around and talk about other people. Gossip about family and neighbors. I am not built that way and this is why I am rarely in their presents when they get together. In addition being a recovered alcoholic I can not be in that environment.

I have come to terms with not feeling guilty for the way I think or feel. I am well aware that my feelings may cause me to think in ways that are irrational. I realize that I can't make decisions based on my feelings because they will be unrealistic. I also know that my feelings should not be downplayed simply because they are so strong and sometimes extreme. I also do not like it when I am told or made to think that I can feel a type of way. For example that famous saying I talked about before: People love to tell you to cherish or respect your mother because you only have one. Last time I checked respect goes both ways and there is only one of everyone. It is ok to feel how you feel. If your feelings get in the way of you making rational decisions then that may cause a problem. If your feelings are justified due to the actions of others including your mother that is ok also. I don't think I should be shamed for having feelings that are not 100% loving and caring to my mother. Just because I don't treat or see her as my God or a God does not mean that I do not love or respect her. I simply am acknowledging that she is human. She is not perfect and it shows.

Addiction is a hard battle to win no matter what the drug of choice is. Once you accomplish the goal of becoming sober from whatever your choice of drug is the battle then becomes staying sober or away from that particular evil. I know from experience. I also know that it can change you as a person. I know you are not the parent you need to be or maybe even want to be and a lot of people go through it. A lot of people don't get help, because they can't or won't. Some think that they are ok without help. I believe my mother is the type that doesn't want help because she believes she is doing fine and she is not an addict. So it makes it hard to communicate with someone who is not willing to help themselves and doesn't want to face their reality. I put this prenotion on her that if I eventually tried to face my demons with her she would not respond in a way that I would like. At the end of the day for my sanity it is no longer about her response but it is more about me doing what I can to get rid of the heavy baggage I have and letting go. In order to do that I have to at least try to release my negative energy by letting her know how I really feel. Until that task is done I will forever be stuck in anger and resentment in relation to her and our relationship.

Writing this book is revealing to me. I believe in

writing to heal and that is exactly what I am doing. This really is a journey through my journal of Mommy issues. Some of my experiences with her have not been the best. Living with her as an adult really turned me off from seeing her as a friend more than I expected. When I got into this living situation I thought it would be the best for me and my family but at times I feel like it has been the biggest headache and caused a dislike for my mother even more. Not just from me but my children also. My daughter confessed to me that she used to think my mother was the nicest grandma and now she just seems crazy and at times very mean.

    I remember one mother's day we had at our house. My mother in law, her friend, my mom, my husband and children were all there. Everyone was drinking except the children of course. We were having a good time. All of a sudden my mother got into this shitty mood. Her attitude changed for the worse. She wanted everything to be about her. My husband was singing a song off the radio to his mother and everyone was enjoying themselves. In the middle of the song my mother changed the radio station and started to complain. No one paid her any attention but that rubbed me the wrong way and I was angry with her for a long time from that day. That was one of the worst mother day celebrations that I had. I never understood why she acted the way that she did. When she gets drunk she is either angry or annoying. Now all drunks can be annoying I know but with my mother it's different. She gets into this child-like mood where everything she says or does is whining, complaining, or emulating a child. It is embarrassing and annoying. Even her best friend who is my God mom witnessed this and told her about herself due to these actions. My God mom is one that does not bite her tongue so when she confronted her in my head I was like "yes somebody needed to say it". You're too damn old to be acting like this.

To this day my mother is constantly getting drunk almost on a day to day basis. She is no longer doing drugs thankfully. Her drunken state usually results in her acting immature or just being inappropriate. The anger has seemed to calm down and she no longer has fits like a toddler. I get irritated with her because it is tiresome and goes on too often for too long now. I wish she had more hobbies other than sitting at home and drinking. A lot of my frustrations with her comes from the disappointment of her not bettering herself or growing. It's like she has given up on life and that is not the Mommy I knew back in the day. She used to love to get out and be social and now she pushes people away or at least it seems that way.

So my teenage years though I really was able to do what I wanted being raised by my Grandma saved me from ruining my life. I would go out every now and again but for the most part I was a homebody or I would stay over a friend's house who also did not care too much about going out. I lived between my Mom-Mom and mom house on and off. I can't really recall the reason behind that, except for the fact that my mother was still into drugs and it wasn't good for me to be around. I got good grades and would go to school everyday even up until the end of the year when the teachers may not have shown. I hated being home when I was living with my mom or Mom Mom.

I do remember during prom and my mom really showing up for me and paying for prom. My mom always did somehow manage to keep a job and money in her pocket.

I am disappointed in my mother. She used to be the type of person that was unstoppable. She seemed like she used to want more for herself even though she had problems. I expected more for her but in my eyes she gave up on herself. When your life only consists of drinking, eating and sleeping that is not living. What type of value for life is that? It kind of hurts to see her get old and never reach her dreams. Everyone has a purpose and I guess hers is giving me content for this book. Maybe her mistakes are to make the next generation better. My mom is not God. It is hard to say that but to contradict that statement God is in everything and everyone. Just because it is not how I expected it or how I wanted it doesn't mean it is not for me. This journey has a lot of emotions tied to it. As you can see writing this book has me figuring out how to manage my emotions related to my relationship with my mother. Even if you claim to hate your mother or feel as if your mother hates you there is still a life lesson in figuring out what has gone wrong. At this point in life I'm just tired of keeping it in. I'm tired of making excuses for who I am. I'm tired of the anger and resentment. It is time to let go and let God. No my mother doesn't owe me anything because I am grown and I am responsible for my own mental health.

Now I can figure out my own issues with my mother and deal with them like an adult but when it comes to my children there is no reason or excuse for how she treats them when I am not around. This part I don't understand. So I have come to the conclusion that she is jealous of the relationship between my daughter and I. In addition after living with my mother my daughter does not get overly excited to see her anymore. My daughter is the type of person that treats people the way they treat her. She doesn't hide the way she feels about a person. So when she is treated unfairly by my mother she acts accordingly. My mom denies the way she treats her which frustrates me even more. One day while drunk as can be she showed her true colors in front of me and my husband. She attempted to talk to my daughter in a mean and nasty manner. I didn't have to say a thing my more level headed other half did but it rubbed me the wrong way. my mother acted like it never happened and never apologized to my daughter or me.

Living with her as an adult has been very eye opening and challenging. Whenever you disagree with her it hurts her feelings and she gets some type of attitude. When you catch her in a lie she denies. We both are so used to running from confrontation that it is all fake smiles when we pass each other or are in the same room. I have dealt with these issues for years and know it is past due to make a change. For my sanity and peace of mind confronting my issues whether or not she responds well is something I need.

I have to admit I am pretty biased when it comes to my feelings and emotions about my mother. I dont have the worst relationship but in the same breath we are not the mother daughter dual that we seem on the outside or that my mother would have everyone to believe. I only see one side of things and mostly see and feel the negative. I am affected in ways that some would not understand. I don't know what goes on in her head. I don't know how she truly feels. I have never asked and if she was to tell me to be quite honest I wouldn't believe her anyway. But I am entitled to my feelings and feel justified for feeling the way that I do.

The real resolve here is to just accept these feelings, confront them and maybe unload my luggage on my mom. But sometimes I'm confused with myself on what type of relationship I want with my mom, and what I really want to do in regards to our relationship. I want to let go and let God. I want to leave our issues in the past. But what does that look like for us? How do we begin?

"Gratitude turns what we have into enough"

Chapter 9

So far I have only shared what I go through as a daughter but I'm a mother. I have suffered from addiction, depresion, anxiety, panic attacks, PTSD and sometimes I still do. I have made broken promises to my children. I have done things and put them in situations that could or have traumatized them. I might have neglected them in ways or made them feel bad or even disrespected them. I am not God. I try my best to be the parent that I thought I needed and the parent that I think they need. I only try to do what's best for them. I take the lessons I have learned and try to apply them to my parenting style. I am only human. I am still growing and so are they. I don't know how my children feel or felt about my decisions and parenting. I know that when I do make these mistakes or feel as if I have somehow wronged my children it eats me up inside. So I try harder and harder to do better by them. I try to make them understand what is going on with me. I give them the opportunity to voice their feelings and opinions. I apologize to them when I know they deserve it. I take my parenting seriously but I also need self discipline and help with my own demons.

My oldest daughter is 13 now and can understand the ways of the world more than my other 2 children. I have a good relationship with her. She enjoys talking to me and being in my presents. I am not just saying this she actually tells me and it is obvious the way she follows me around. I think our only problem is that I can at times cross the boundary of mother daughter versus friends. She does not get disrespectful or out of place but I know it is certain things I don't need to talk to her about but I do. A friend is not what she needs from me at this point in her life. She needs a companion in me to talk and learn from and someone she can trust who can offer advice to things she deals with as a teenager. To sit up and gossip with her or try to make it seem like we are at the same level in life is not important or helpful for her growth. So I try to keep teaching her to guide her and support her without any confusion. Sometimes I slip up because she is fun to be around and easy to talk to. When I notice my mistakes I try not to make them again and I also communicate this with her.

My style of parenting consists of a lot of conversation that is something I didn't really get from my mother. A lot of what she should have been teaching and telling me I had to learn elsewhere. For example, a young woman is supposed to be able to go to Mommy when it comes to that time of the month. Not only did I not know what was going on when it happened I turned to a friend of the same age to get information about the do's and don'ts. The first time I spotted my mom kind of brushed it off because it wasn't the full period so I was told to do nothing about it. When I did begin to bleed for real her exact words were "oh your period on you need a pad". It was no sit down and talk about it. I just knew I was bleeding and I guess it was normal. When I went to school and went to the bathroom I took my pad off thinking that was ok. My friend had to tell me otherwise and I had to find out through her and other resources about what not to do.

This is why I talk to my children. I don't want them getting information that may or may not be true from outside influences. I want them to be able to talk to me about whatever they feel is necessary. I want my daughter to be comfortable with our relationship and I want to be comfortable that she is making good decisions when I am not around.

Respect, Honor, and Cherish your mother was all I heard growing up. But shouldn't we offer these same things to our children? I am a strong believer in respect going both ways. Respect should not be determined by your age, position, or by the fact that you birthed a child. Respect should be given no matter who you are. My mom means a lot to me. My mother should also respect me because I am a human just like her. I really dislike when people try to shame me for my feelings toward my mom. If my mom disrespects me to a point of no end am I still to respect her?

Now as a mature adult I know how to be civil towards others even if I'm disrespected so I am not really asking these questions to be a rebel. I just am not a fan in telling others to not feel how they feel about what they go through when it comes to mommy. It's like the world wants you to bow down to someone who may not even look at you with a loving heart. Kiss the ass of someone just because they birth you. I wasn't asked to be born and Mommy wasn't the only one who was involved in me being here or being the person that I am. You only get one mom, one dad, one God, you only get one of every one. All these cliche montras about Mommy are not for everyone. They make some people feel guilty for having feelings and having a different experience than the next person. I respect her but I don't like or appreciate the things she has and is putting me through. I don't appreciate the toxicity that she brings to me and my family. I don't appreciate the dishonesty, the neglect, or heartache. I didn't know how to feel about it, how to deal with it, or how to respond to it. I am entitled to be angry, upset, emotional, and opinionated about what I have been through. This does not mean I don't respect, cherish, or honor my mother.

"Knowledge will give you power but character respect_Bruce Lee"

Chapter 10

One of the main components to a working relationship is trust. All parties of a relationship have to have some level of trust. Trust that the other will not mislead or misguide them in any way. Trust that they are there to better them and not tear them down or cause harm purposely. The level of trust I have in my mother is very little. Before I really paid any attention to her behavior and actions trust wasn't an issue. I would assume that she had my best interest in heart. I would assume she wanted the best for me and wanted to see me succeed. I thought she would want to see me happy by any means. She provided for me whatever I needed and most of what I wanted for the years I couldn't provide for myself as a child and teen. When the adult years of my life hit and we lived together it was as if she was and is jealous of something so she doesnt want me to be or do my best.

For example whenever someone tells her about me or talks about me she tends to catch a negative attitude and doesn't want to hear what they have to say. If I personally go to her to tell her about myself her response feels fake and she lacks interest in my life. I like to talk about goals and aspirations and she seems to brush that off as if it is not something she is into. I know the feeling of being a parent and a child comes to you talking about a musician that you know nothing about and really don't care too much to learn about them. But as a parent you listen anyway and maybe ask a question or two about this person. A child just appreciates a listening ear. A child just likes to get off their mind what they have been thinking about all day sometimes it doesn't even matter if you are listening just as long as they are talking. We are grown now so you would think that grown ups can talk about topics that have meaning. Talking about goals and things that interest them you know have real conversations. Not my mother. When I do sit around and talk to her she more or less likes to talk about people and more so in a negative manner.

Fear is a word we live with everyday. Fear comes up in relationships all the time. I fear making someone mad or sad. I fear the other person will leave me or hate me. My fear with my mother is that I will upset her. She seems to be so sensitive on the surface that at times I feel I need to tiptoe around her. She doesn't like confrontation especially when sober. That trait has also rubbed off and been passed down to me. With the guidance of my husband and therapist I have come to the realization that confrontation is not all bad. Fear is not all bad. Confronting someone you love on an issue that you constantly think about or that upsets me is actually a healthy step to restoring a broken relationship. The response of the person is not something I have control over and should not stop me from releasing my pain. My fear is something that I should and have been using lately as fuel to better my life. I fear her getting angry, cussing, and yelling but it's not like she will hate me. She will never stop loving me. I know that she just doesn't know the proper way to deal with emotions so she does what she knows best. I know that she may be smarter than what she put on at times. So after the smoke clear she will go back to asking for kisses.

What I don't know is if me confronting her about my issues with her will change her. But that is ok. I know I did my part and tried my best. I know I will no longer have a monkey on my back or walk around on eggshells just to satisfy her craziness. I also fear timing. When is the right time to discuss something that you know will make someone upset? When is the right time to tell someone that years ago that they were not the best to them? Or that you've been hurting for years because of their actions or lack of? How do you deliver bad news at any given time? I think too much into details and it places these fears into my mind. In reality it's never a right time to do anything and fear is not real.

"I don't trust people who don't love themselves and tell me I love you....There is a African saying which is: Be careful when a naked person offers you a shirt_Maya Angelou

Chapter 11

Some Mothers are receptive to constructive criticism. Some Mothers are stuck in their ways but still will try to hear you out. Then you have some who will not listen because they think they know best and no one can tell them otherwise.

There are 4 generations of us with totally different relationships. The further down the line you go the better the relationship. My Mom-Mom and mother have to be the most dysfunctional and difficult to understand. My mother and I did a little better but a lot of collateral damage. My daughter and I are still growing but headed in the right direction. Now the mixture of relationships are even worse. I feel like my Mom-Mom hates me for some reason I will get into that a little later. My daughter and Mom Mom have a non existing relationship. My mom seems like she dislikes my daughter behind the scenes but loves her in public. As for my daughter she is very nonchalant about those two and adores me. I am not God to my daughter.

My Mom-Mom seems like she dislikes me very much and I think a part of it is because I won't let her talk to me like a child. I won't let her manipulate me or buy my affection and I never have. She thinks I am naive and that she knows more than me so I am unable to tell her anything. She calls me disrespectful when I simply tell her how I feel or don't want to hear what she has to say because it's mostly negative. She is an energy draining person to be around. I could only imagine my mother's childhood looking at how they are now with each other.

No my Mom-Mom does not really have much of a relationship with my children. That is fine because I dont expect no one to care for them but me and their dad. She buys them little things here and there or gives them money because I guess that's what she knows. As far as them spending time together I really don't approve because she can be negative and inappropriate. At times she will tell my children that they need to get their hair done or need to fix this or do that. She won't say it in a nice way or offer to help but she makes sure you know she doesn't approve. My Mom-Mom once bought my oldest daughter a sewing machine so she can start getting into designing clothes. When showing her how to use it something suddenly went wrong with this brand new machine. We haven't seen it since then. She used the same machine to alter the dresses for my wedding but never gave it back to my daughter. Not sure what that was about but we didn't ask for it in the first place. If the gift isn't genuine we don't want it.

I repeat my mother's mistakes at times and knowing this scares me the most. I try to learn from them, change the outcome and break the generational curse.

Becoming like your Mother as you get older can be a blessing and a curse to many. We are taught to not trust other females because they may be jealous or hurt us. So as a mother raising a young woman do you not trust her? Are our Mother's the only woman we should trust and not everyone else? How exactly does this work? What needs to be taught is that everyone hurts and everyone gets hurt. It can be intentional or accidental but you will get hurt. What matters is how you perceive it, how you interpret it and how you handle it. We need some type of brain reset on how to treat each other. My hurt from my mother is unintentional. I can logically say that my mother is not out to hurt me. I read somewhere couples that argue love each other more. Confronting someone about my feelings may hurt but the pain that they caused either on purpose or unintentionally does not have to be as difficult as I make it. My mother has been the number one person that I have this problem with. Why? I'm not sure myself. I have grown enough to come to an understanding that I am allowed to express myself especially if I am being wronged or hurt somehow. But why is it I hold back when checking my mother if I want to grow and want her to understand how I feel. A part of it might be fear of hurting her feelings. This woman who was once my God. I believe that I will crush her or make her hate me. I don't want to put an even bigger strain on our relationship, especially when we live in the same house and her interactions with my children on a day to day basis might change. I guess I am afraid of confrontation. I know it's a possibility that this will not turn out the way my brain thinks it will; but am I willing to take that risk for my sanity? If my mother was to take anything I say in a negative way instead of just hearing me out and hearing my hurt then I guess it would mean she is still stuck in a dysfunctional mindset and I pretty much can't do anything about that. I can just leave it where it is knowing I did my best.

I thank God for my sub mothers. The woman in my life that played that motherly role that I needed. Starting with my grandmother, (my father's mother) who took me in for years as my mother worked on getting her life together. My grandma humbled me and taught me what was important to survive in this world. She opened my eyes to things most children don't get to see being poor and black from the inner city of Philadelphia. We would go to all types of museums and events in the city. She would have me watching the olympics and of course routing for everyone black person. She would tell me about my history of where we came from. She showed me good work ethics. She educated me outside of the school system. She made sure I stayed out of trouble. We went to church and my favorite were the holidays and family reunions. We would cook everything from scratch. No cans and boxes over here. I may have mentioned this before but I do praise and thank her a lot. I am pretty sure she had her downfalls but I was either too young to see them or she hid them very well. She was one of those old school grandmoms and I know that's what makes me different then most women.

Then I have my God mom. From what I know when my mom was out and about my God mom made sure I wanted for nothing. She took care of me when my mom was occupied. She made sure I had everything I needed even if they were not getting along at the time. I remember being younger and hanging out with her sometimes. I remember babysitting her son who is about 7 years younger than me. Back then he was a badass. My God mom seemed to always have her life together and knew who and what she was. I know this is not always true with us women but it sure did look like it on the surface. She is one of the ones who always kept a job, a house or apartment and a car. She was always dressed to impress and didn't need anyone for nothing but was there when you needed her.

I also had Aunts that were my mom's friends and not really related. I had neighbors, my friends' moms, my mother in law etc. Each and every one of these ladies in my life and has something to do with who I am today. I have special relationships with them and I appreciate them all.

Don't get me wrong, everyone has their flaws and I didn't always understand or appreciate the lessons that came along with these relationships. As I grow I learn to look at the positives and recognize the lessons that are being taught. Being a mother is a difficult job and to take in someone as your child on top of having your own or already having raised your own is something that is taken for granted at times. So I am grateful for these women.

My mother in law has been in my life since I was about 14 years old. She took me in and treated me like her own from the start. I have had my ups and downs with her as if she was my real mother. At one point my mother in law and I struggled to get along. We were alike in a lot of ways and totally opposite in other ways. We had the old school spirit of the way you took care of home. For example we always said how the main rooms in your house that should stay clean were the kitchen and bathroom. We both love to cook and the big mammas house type feels on Sundays. I gravitated towards my husband's family so much because they were so family oriented. While my family was pretty distant and small on my mother's side. Their family was always big and just like they took me in they took everyone else in.

This reminded me of what I was missing from my time being raised by my grandmother. She was loving and welcoming if she liked you but she was also strong headed and very opinionated. We bumped heads over the little things. She was the type of person if you brought something to her attention that you didn't agree with she would hear you and change if she knew you were right. If you were wrong in her eyes that was a different story she was not trying to hear a thing.

My mother's friend Terri who I consider another mother of mine is very special to me also. She helps when it comes to keeping my mom tamed. She is someone I can talk to about my mom when either one of us gets frustrated by her antics. I believe my mother is jealous of the conversations we hold and the bond we have built. Whenever she is told about a conversation that we had she gets upset and doesn't want to hear it. My second mother and I have more of an empowering relationship. We try to encourage each other and like to share the good news with one another. She has been a part of my life for a very long time and she is as sweet as can be. I know that if I needed her she would be right there by my side. I actually call on her before my own mother. It's sad that we actually have to sneak and have conversations due to my mother's reaction to our relationship.

My daughter and I have a special relationship for now and I hope it stays this way. She is comfortable coming to me telling me mostly anything and everything. I am very open with my daughter. I like to explain to her what I go through as a mother and as a woman. I express to her the difficulties about my depression, addiction, my goals and just being human. I listen to her and try to engage when she talks about anything and everything. My daughter is more like her father than she is like me and I think that is another reason we get along. I mean he is my best friend. She is growing so beautifully and is a respectful young lady. I think being transparent with our children makes it easier to be a parent. Letting them know that we once were all children and we all made these same mistakes. We make mistakes now that we still have to clean up.

My relationship with my mom used to be a good one when I was young. I adored her as if she were my own mother. I remember when she would get dressed in her fancy clothes and put on her perfume I would be right up under her playing dress up. I thought it was so amazing the way she would dress and carry herself. I used to think she was rich and had it all. At the time I was the only grandchild so of course I was the favorite. I lived with my Mom-Mom off and on throughout my years. We got along pretty well until I started to spend more time with my husbands (than boyfriends) family. I think my family has and has a real jealousy problem.

A part of my anxiety of being a mother or just a woman period is not being any better than the previous generations. I resist the thought of taking on my mother's not so good traits that at times it consumes me and I am doing exactly what I don't want to do. When I focus on what I don't want too much it is like I am calling it to action. I am bringing it into my life without even realizing it. So in order to avoid this I really try to listen when I am told I am acting out of character or seem like I am miserable. I try to pay attention to the way I react to my mother. I do self care in order to concentrate on me and not on the negative around me. If I focus on the positive then that is what I will get positivity. I have battled with alcohol addiction for a long time. When I used to drink it was a fun experience at the time and my excuses for doing it were reasonable when I was younger. Having children while drinking or should I say overindulging in alcohol was the problem. Being annoying, being a totally different person while on alcohol is that person in my mother that I didn't want to become. Yet I found myself doing just that. At least in my head, I felt like I was just like her. Maybe not as annoying and I never got angry but I was sloppy and embarrassing at times. I would fall all over the place, get emotional, reveal a side of me that was not appropriate for my children or family and friends to see. I would have little to no memory of what I did or said. I lost time and memories because of it. My mom does these things way too often. We have to pretend as if she doesn't do anything because she won't remember the next day. We have to just ignore how annoying she is because we know she is drunk. I usually end up telling my children that she is just crazy so ignore her. I know that's not right but I really don't know what else to say.

I have never once thought or said to myself I hope I dont be like my mother or I don't want to become my mother. It is more or less the negative versus the positive. What I see in her that is not so good I want to shy away from but not make it my main concern. I want to keep the positive and pass it on. The mother daughter relationship is a tricky one from generation to generation but it is a relationship that needs more attention and that needs to be talked about a lot more. These relationships can teach us or turn us into monsters and no one realizes the true impact this one relationship has on our lives. Society is so quick to call a man a dead beat dad for leaving the child and no one wants to talk about the dead beat mom. Mommy is not God.

If fixing this cycle of broken mother daughter relationships is something you can see yourself doing a good place to start is writing. When I started this journey I was stuck on leaving everything as is. I felt like it would be pointless and I just needed to get away from those I felt was not making my life better. I realized that I have never tried. I keep everything I go through to myself and expect it to get better or go away. I have come to a lot of realizations about myself. I know that fixing my relationship with my mother or at the very least letting her know how I feel is not for her but it is a part of my growth. I know that if I at least try that I did everything I could in order to better the situation. The writing was half of the journey which has allowed me to open up and admit all that I felt, feel and have been through. I just hope and pray to at least be at peace with my relationship with my mother.

Some relationships are broken beyond the point of resurrection. The negativity, name calling, abuse, and toxic behavior of the relationship may already be too far gone to mend. That is perfectly fine. If that's the case then work on yourself and know that you did everything in your power to right your wrongs.

We as women, especially black women need to stick together. Mothers need to show and teach our daughter how to be princesses and one day black queens. a Mother daughter relationship doesn't stop in the home. It continues outside in our community through our sub mothers. We need to do more uniting than dividing. It is ok to compliment other sista or offer a helping hand. It is ok to ask for help. I want all my black queens to lead these young princesses in the right direction. We all can truly win. I'm tired of the hate, anger, and fights.

I hope sharing my story brings change to at least one person. If so I have completed my goal. I need us as black women to heal and grow stronger. We need each other and I am ok with admitting that. We can only hope and pray that our mothers did and are doing the best they can with the hand they have been dealt. We can only hope and pray that we don't one mess our children up as badly as we have been messed up. That we do better with each generation moving forward. We are great, we just need to show it and use our greatness for good not evil. Our mothers love and hurt us at the same time. They prepare us for this world, the good and the bad. We can't ask for her to do more than what she is capable of or less than expected. We have to hold ourselves accountable for the part we play in the relationship and move on if necessary. We have to give the baggage of hurt to the right person in order to move on. Just keep in mind mommy is not God. If you Don't expect her to be and you won't be let down as much.

"Don't judge my choices without understanding my reasons"

Poem Part 2 by Ayanna Dixon

I'm your child, you spawn a replica of you!

I tell you I love you

Care for you and what i say is true

I tell you that I only want the best

So why do you treat me like shit?

Are you putting me to the test?

Are you questioning my love and admiration for you

So you don't give me any?

Are you so caught up in your own little world

That you make excuses, cause i can think of plenty

Plenty of reasons as to why I should leave

But I stay,

I stay because I want so badly for you to love me

When I told you what you did

You didn't even believes

A lot of times I wonder

Do you even see me?

The Author

"Tacarra Braxton" who writes under the pen name **CARRA DIXON** grew up in Philadelphia Pa.

Facing many adversities from abuse, neglect, drugs and alcohol Dixon's voice was silenced. As a way to express herself, Dixon's love for writing was born. Poems, journaling, and storytelling became her passion. Dixon contributes her most impressionable years to her paternal Grandmother who taught her confidence, pride, and strength amongst other things as a young black girl. Today Dixon's passion is to instill in young girls what her grandma did in her.

Dixon's goal is to build a community of empowered black girls that no one can tear down or silence. Dixon is starting this with one book at a time because our voices collectively will be heard.

When Dixon's isn't writing and advocating for young girls she enjoys mothering her two daughters and son, and being a wife.

www.ingramcontent.com/pod-product-compliance
Lightning Source LLC
Chambersburg PA
CBHW071139090426
42736CB00012B/2173